Can we regard our life as a uselessly disturbing episode in the blissful repose of nothingness?

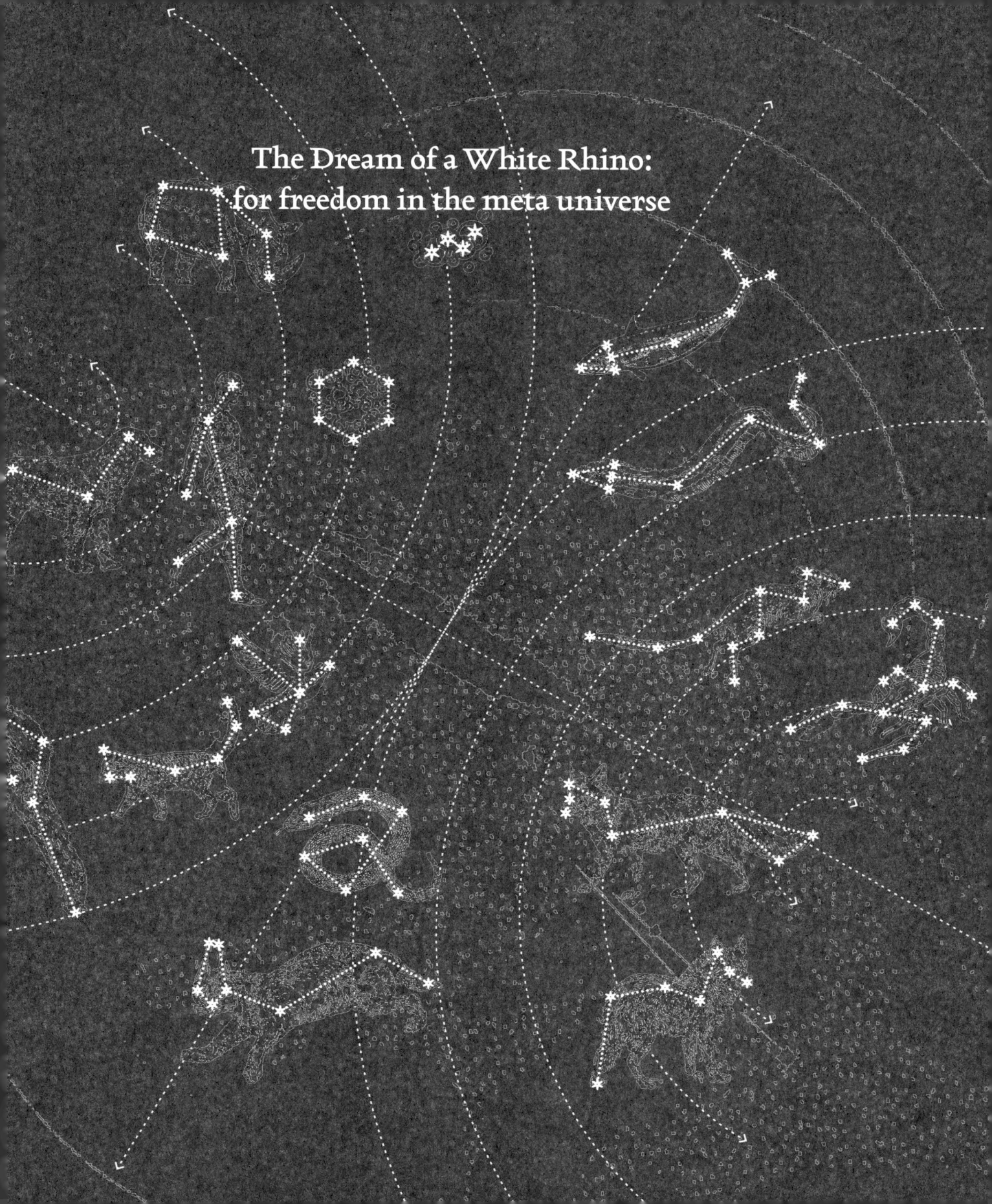

I A Long Beginning	5	V An Uncomfortable Reunion	95
II Separate Destinies	19	VI Land of Lights	119
III The King of the Desert	45	VII Happy Sleep	143
IV A Fierce Guy	69	VIII Awakening	163

I

A Long Beginning

It was just a small bubble.

Nobody knows how long it was there.
Since the bubble was unaware of its existence,
it couldn't sense the passage of time.

In the surrounding endless darkness,
for a very long time,
nothing revealed itself.

There was nothing and nothing happened,
so everything was extremely quiet
and exceptionally peaceful.

I

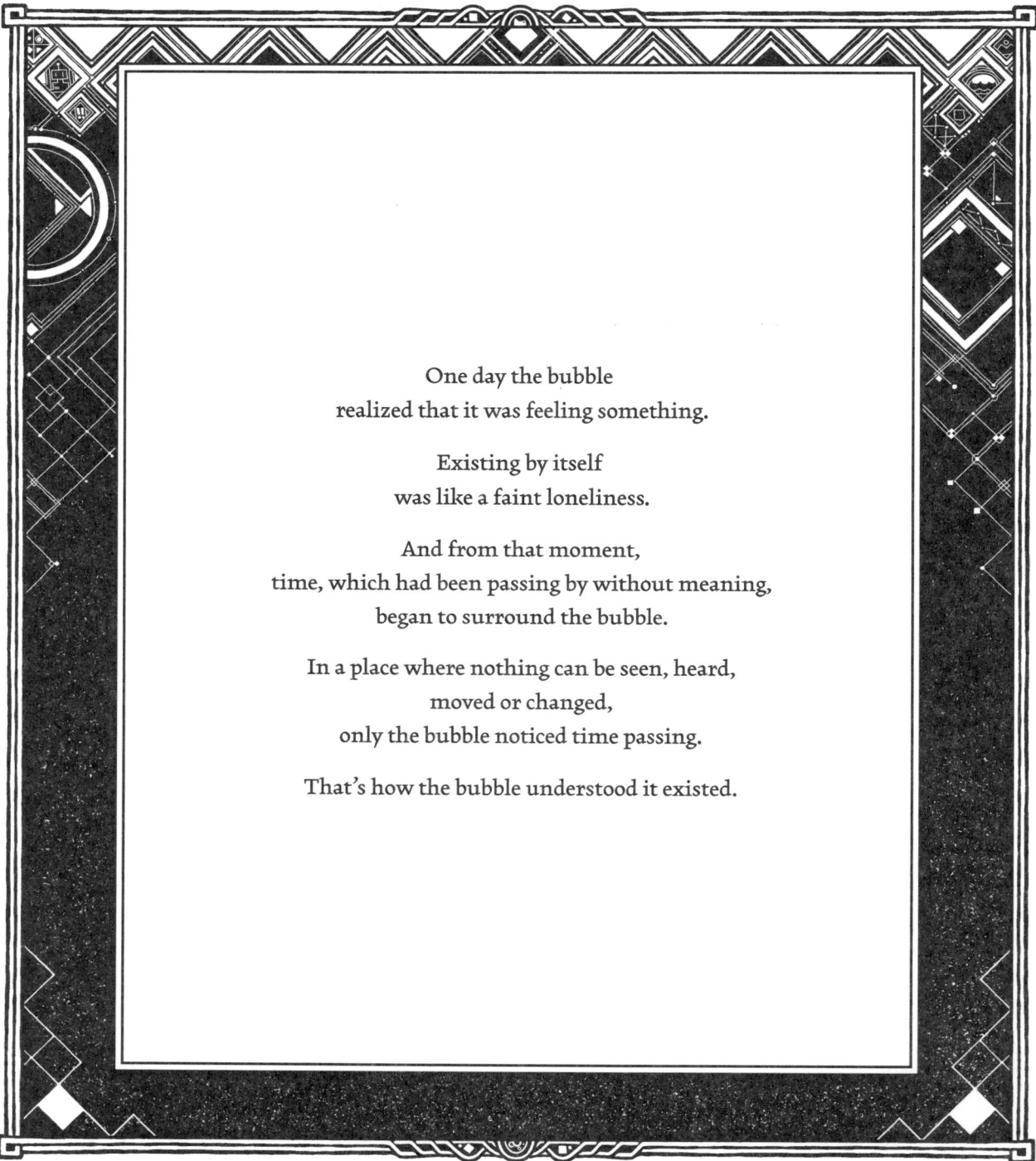

One day the bubble
realized that it was feeling something.

Existing by itself
was like a faint loneliness.

And from that moment,
time, which had been passing by without meaning,
began to surround the bubble.

In a place where nothing can be seen, heard,
moved or changed,
only the bubble noticed time passing.

That's how the bubble understood it existed.

A Long Beginning

And one day, after a long time had passed,
the bubble tried to move its body a little.

It was just a small tremor at first.
There wasn't any direction to it.

Because in the darkness where there's nothing,
you can't tell the difference between this way and that way.

But the bubble, little by little, began to imagine.

As the tremor grew into a shaking,
the movements forward and backward,
left and right, and up and down, got longer,
and as the speed increased,
it realized that maybe there's something more
than this seemingly infinite darkness.

I

The bubble didn't hate the quiet darkness
it was familiar with.

But it wanted to see something other than darkness.

Because there was nothing,
there was nothing to see, nothing to hear,
nothing to bump into.
It wasn't even aware of these senses, but it thought,

"Since I'm here,
there must be something out there somewhere.
It could be anything."

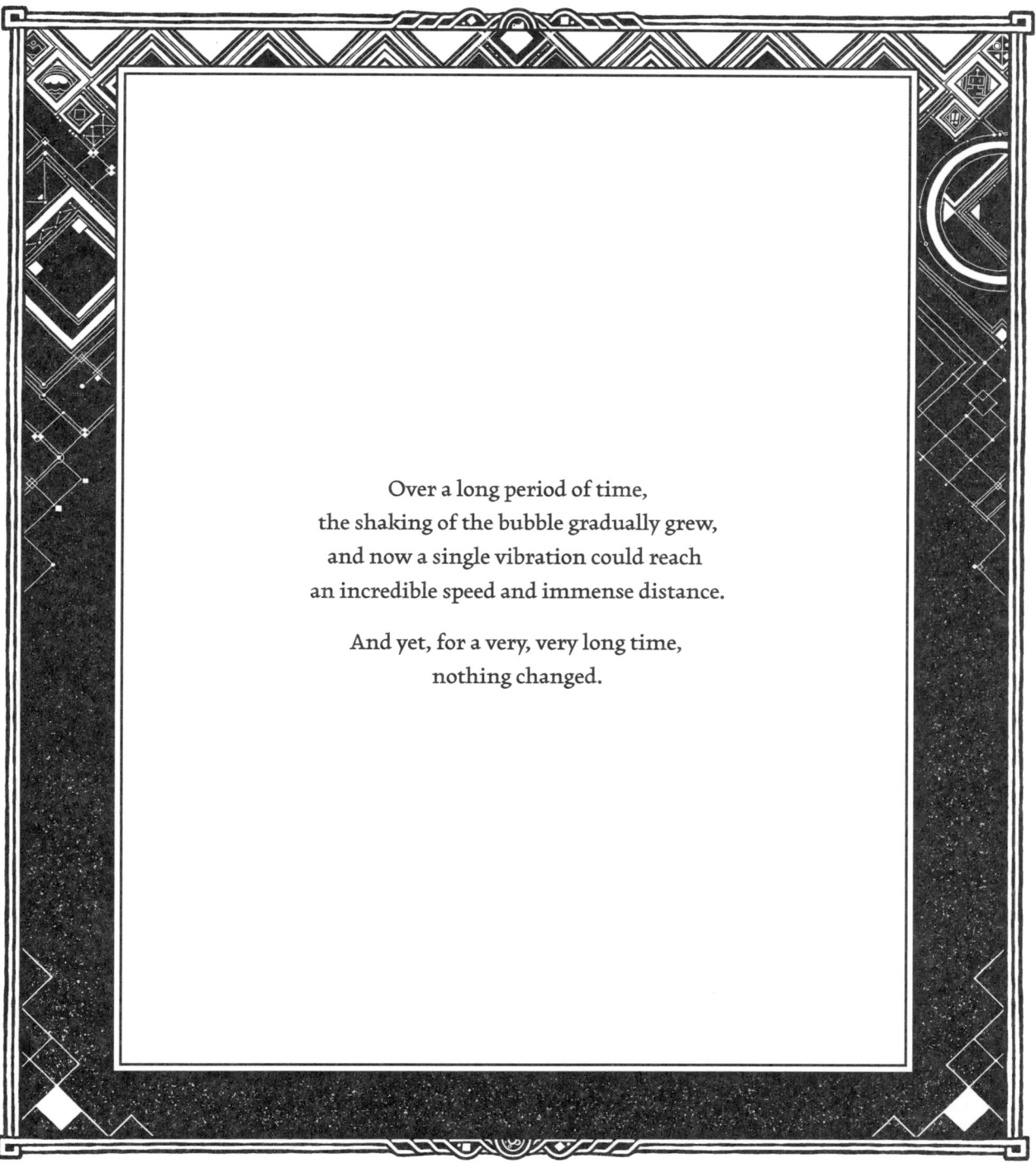

Over a long period of time,
the shaking of the bubble gradually grew,
and now a single vibration could reach
an incredible speed and immense distance.

And yet, for a very, very long time,
nothing changed.

The first time the bubble saw something
must've been the moment
when it was just about to give up.

The moment something other than darkness appeared,
it finally learned what it meant to see.

It was very far and faint,
but in the infinite darkness of space and time,
it was something the bubble couldn't and wouldn't miss.
It was a dot of pale blue light

I

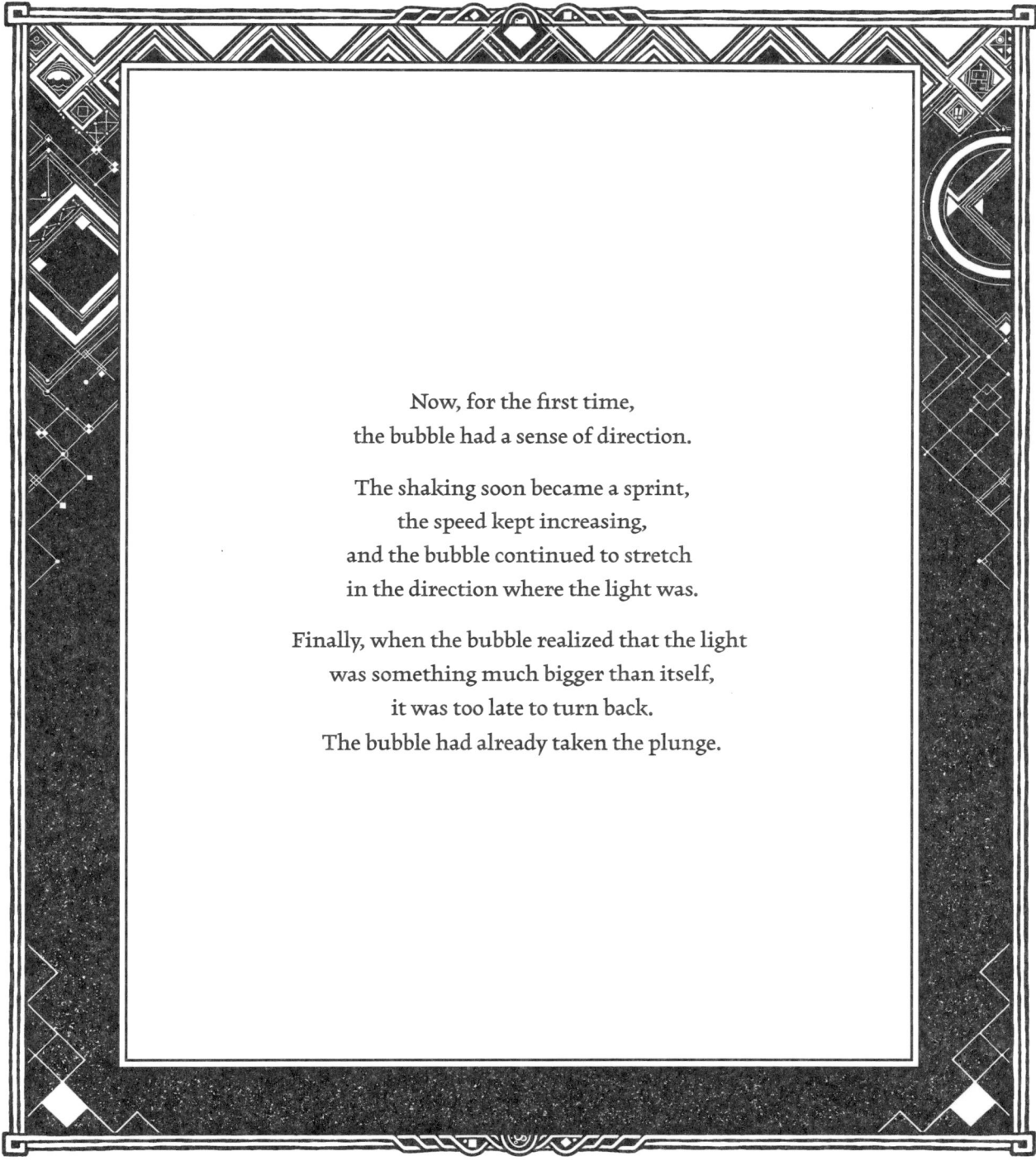

Now, for the first time,
the bubble had a sense of direction.

The shaking soon became a sprint,
the speed kept increasing,
and the bubble continued to stretch
in the direction where the light was.

Finally, when the bubble realized that the light
was something much bigger than itself,
it was too late to turn back.
The bubble had already taken the plunge.

II

 Separate Destinies

Splash!

He fell into the sea.
He wasn't a round bubble anymore.

Now he was small and long,
and had fins on his back, sides, and on his tail.
He became a blue fish.

Freedom in the air was complete freedom, but freedom in the sea was wonderful.

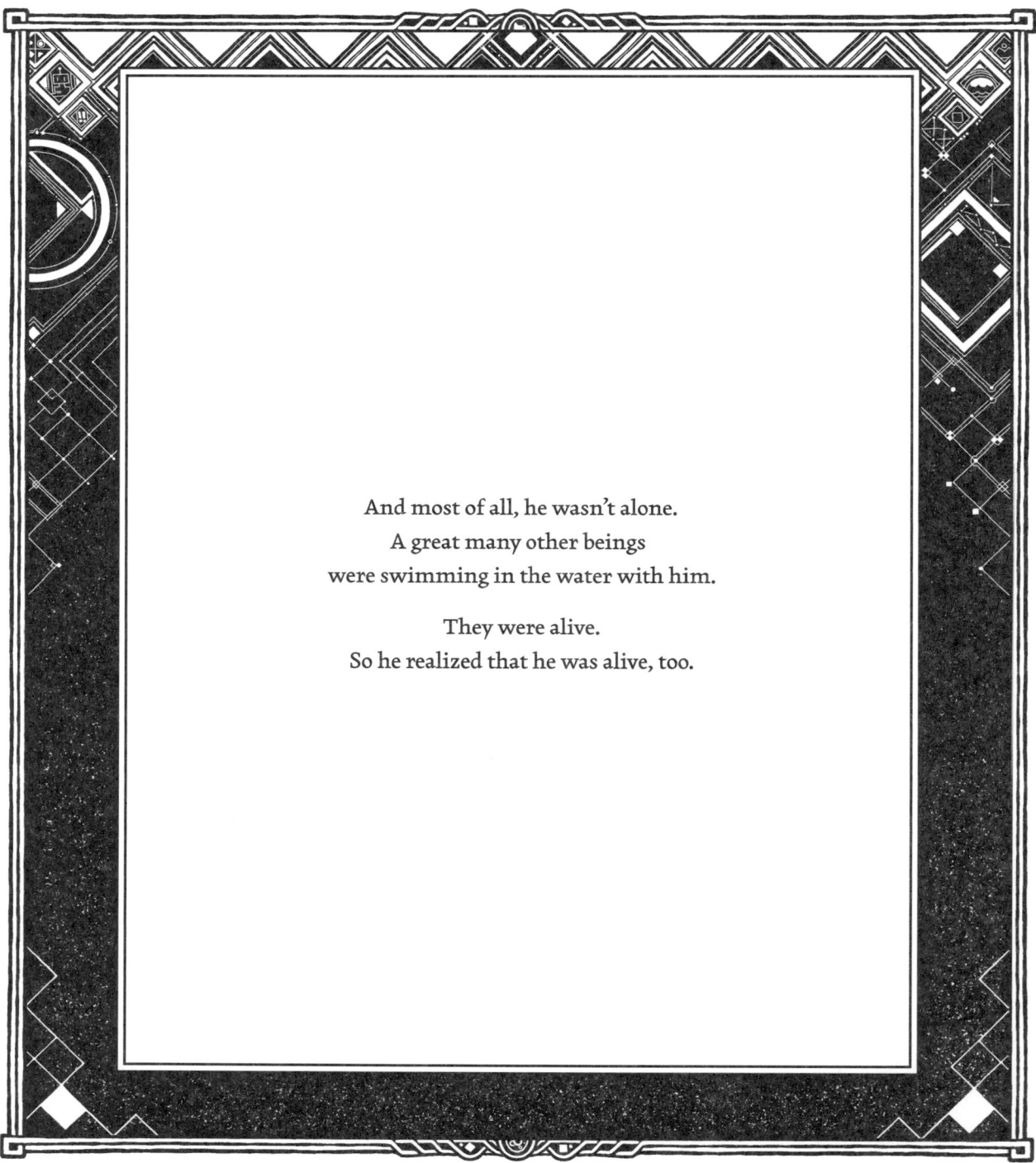

And most of all, he wasn't alone.
A great many other beings
were swimming in the water with him.

They were alive.
So he realized that he was alive, too.

The sea was a dazzling and busy place.
He swam without stopping.

He dove down deep and rose to the shallows.
He slid between the sprouting seaweed,
watched all kinds of similar-looking yet different creatures,
followed the smaller ones,
and deftly avoided the larger ones.

Passing quickly by him
a long, strange thing muttered,

"Get out of the way."

But the strange creature wasn't in a hurry for long.
Suddenly, it stood still in its place.

"Oh, what should I do..."

The long-necked creature was looking around.
It seemed like it didn't know where to go.
The fish stared at it quietly.

He was reminded that just a little while ago
he was also just like the strange creature
wandering around in the dark.

The fish asked the creature,

"What's wrong?"

He was a little surprised at himself
for trying to communicate with
something for the first time.
The creature turned around and spoke coldly.

"Even if I told you, you wouldn't know.
Because you aren't an eel."

"What is an eel?"

The eel stared at the fish like it was pathetic.

"Me. I'm an eel."

II

The eel turned its head again.
Then it stood still, unable to go anywhere.

"I have to go quickly."

The fish swam toward the eel.
For the first time,
he was curious about someone's intentions.

"Where are you going?"

The eel sighed.

"I have to go to the land. But I think I'm lost."

He was going to ask the eel what land was,
but he felt like he'd be treated like an idiot again,
so he changed the question.

"Why do you have to go to the *land*?"

"Why? Because everyone goes there."

"Everyone?"

"Everyone already left. I'm the only one who got lost."

The helpless-looking eel continued to speak.

"When we are born, we have to go to the land.
And then we have to come back to lay eggs.
I was lost in thought for a moment,
it was really only for a moment,
and I ended up losing the group."

"What were you thinking about?"

"I was thinking that I didn't know what *land* was.
I've never seen it. I've never heard of it.
And I don't know what to do there."

"Then why are you going?"

"That's why I stopped to think about why I had to go."

"If you don't know, then you don't have to go, right?"

"Don't say that!"

The fish was startled by the loud cry.

"If I don't go, I have no reason to live.
Because it's fate."

The fish started to feel frustrated.

"But you don't even know what to do.
Isn't that why you stopped? To not go?"

The eel seemed angry.

"No! I just wanted to know the reason.
I was going to rush there once I found out."

The eel's big, round eyes turned red.

"But... Now I'm here alone like this..."

Studying the eel's face the fish asked carefully,

"Is the place called *land* so small that it's difficult to find?
Can't you go there on your own?"

"No, the land is huge.
I have to find the river where my mother used to live.
Don't ask me why.
Eels have been living like this for a very long time.
I wish I hadn't thought about pointless things…"

The eel bit its lip for a moment
and then looked back at the fish with a stern face.

"I don't know the way, but I have to get there somehow.
Sorry I yelled at you. Bye."

The eel quickly bid farewell to the fish,
puffed up its body,
and glided away.

Fate?

Something you absolutely have to do?
Having to go somewhere without knowing why?
That eel is so frustrating and stupid.

But what about me?

"Why did I come here?"

I was looking for something too.
Just like the eel, I didn't know why.
And then the place I arrived at was this sea.

The fish felt that
he also needed the *next thing*.

Until a little while ago, he knew nothing
except darkness, light, and the sea,
but since he discovered a new path,

he decided to follow the way
of the eel and its foolish fate.

I'll go to the land.

II

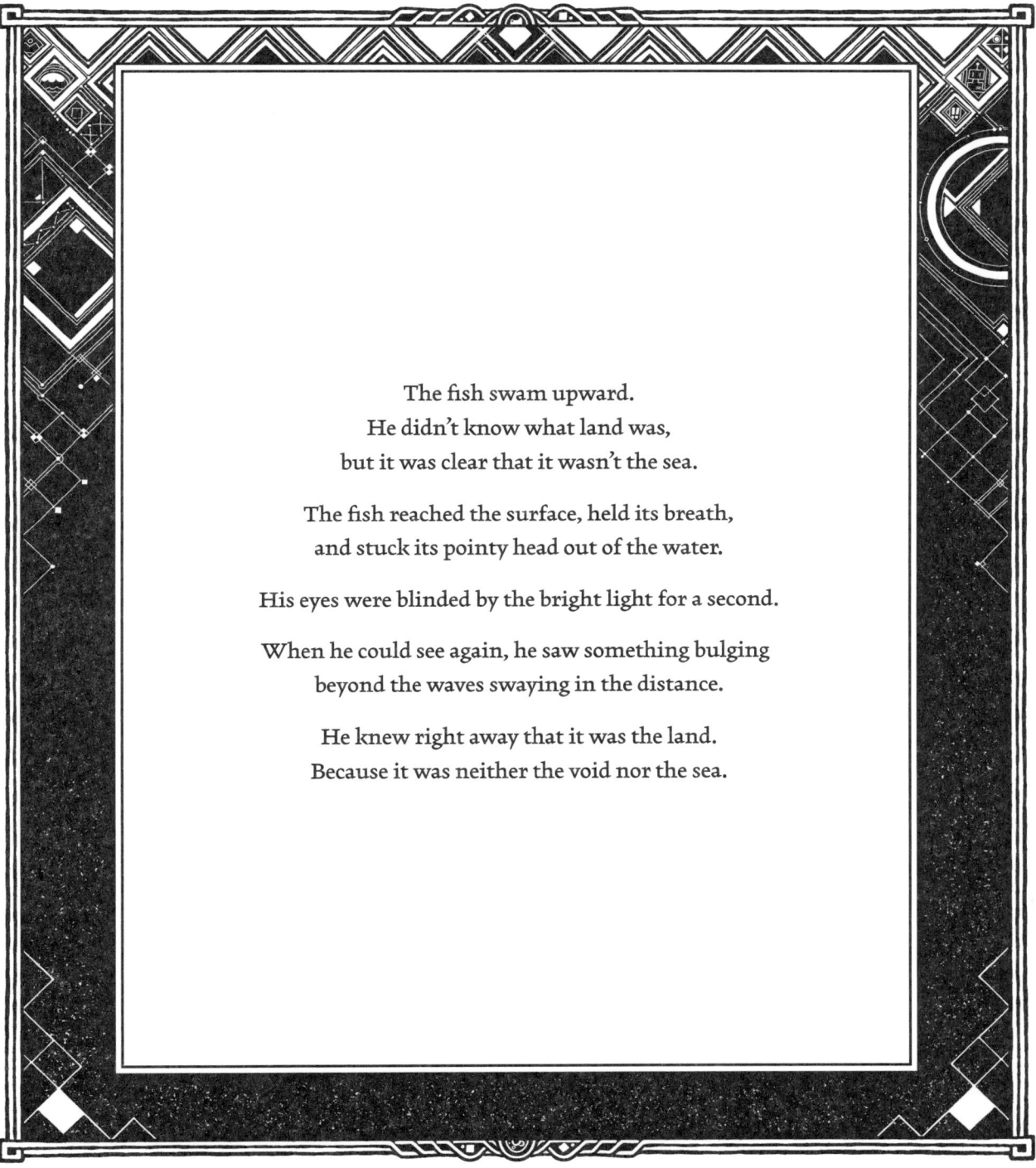

The fish swam upward.
He didn't know what land was,
but it was clear that it wasn't the sea.

The fish reached the surface, held its breath,
and stuck its pointy head out of the water.

His eyes were blinded by the bright light for a second.

When he could see again, he saw something bulging
beyond the waves swaying in the distance.

He knew right away that it was the land.
Because it was neither the void nor the sea.

The fish was amazed and happy to see it.
He swam hard toward land.

But even though it didn't seem far away,
the fish swam and swam, but he couldn't reach it.
Little by little the fish became exhausted.

And then, when the fish thought,

"Oh, maybe I'm getting a little closer,"

he fainted.

III

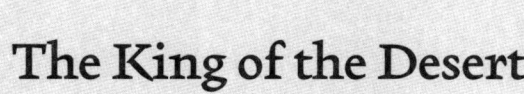
The King of the Desert

III

Splash, splash.

Startled by the sound of the waves,
he opened his eyes.

He was now out of the water,
but he wasn't suffocating.

He was puzzled for a moment,
then he realized that he had four legs.

He was neither a bubble nor a fish,
but a small yellow rat.

He got up and raised his head.

He saw the night sky for the first time.
It was full of small dots of light and a huge lump of light.

Without those lights, the night sky would've been
very similar to the empty space he had left.

The mouse, who had been looking at the sky for a while,
now turned his eyes to his feet.

There was more sand piled up under his little feet
than there were lights in the sky.

"This must be land!"

The mouse tried walking on the sand.
Slowly, then a little faster.
Then he started to run.
His short, neat fur fluttered in the cool breeze.

Indeed, the land was such an amazing place
that the eels came to find it despite the difficult journey.

Not floating and being pulled down by the ground
were feelings he had never felt before,
different feelings from being in the sea.

After running for a while, the mouse sat down on a small sand hill and gazed out toward the sea he had left.

The colors of the sky were changing!

What was once darkish blue gradually turned red,
and then a blazing thing appeared at the far end of the sea.

It gradually took on a round shape,
changing its color from red to yellow,
and rose slowly into the sky.

Now the empty space where only he existed was gone.
This world was a place full of all kinds of things.

III

After watching the sun rise for a while,
the mouse got up and started walking slowly again.

It was very bright now
and all he could see was a vast sand field.

If this is land, what can eels who live in the water do here?

Just then, as the mouse was thoughtlessly
heading toward the other side of the sea,
something suddenly popped out of the sand in front of him.

It was a strange thing with a very small body. It was less than half
his size and it had a flashy color similar to sand.

It lowered its body and raised its tail.

"Don't come any closer."

It spoke with a growl.

"I'm a scorpion. I have poison.
If you think I'm funny and underestimate me because I'm small,
you'll be in big trouble!"

The King of the Desert

III

The mouse stopped and answered.

"Sorry. I don't think you're funny."

The scorpion made its tail stand up and glared at the mouse.

"What? You don't?"

The mouse studied the scorpion carefully.

"No, I don't. I'm also not scared of you."

"..."

The scorpion was silent for a moment.

Then, once again, it put its tail up.

"Watch out for my poison! If you try to eat me..."

"I don't find you funny or scary.
And I have no intention of eating you."

The scorpion who had been scowling at the mouse slowly lowered its tail as if it lost strength.

"Who are you?"

"Me? I'm..."

He looked down at his short, scrawny paws.

"I'm a mouse."

"If you aren't going to eat me, what are you doing here?"

"I was looking for land. This is land, right?"

The scorpion nodded.

"Yes. But this is a desert."

"Desert? Not land?"

"It is, but it's a desert. Are you stupid?"

The scorpion snorted and continued.

"Look. The land is made up of two places.
Forests and deserts. This is the desert. Where I rule."

"What is a forest?"

The scorpion suddenly propped its claws up high
and spoke excitedly.

"There is water in the forest. And trees, too!"

III

The mouse was puzzled.

"Water? There's also a lot of water
in the sea down there."

The scorpion gave a snort.

"That's undrinkable water.
It's dead water. But in the forest…"

"In the forest?"

"There's a stream. There's plenty of water to drink
whenever you're thirsty!"

Then the scorpion gulped.

"In the forest no one gets thirsty like me."

After hearing what the scorpion said,
the mouse felt thirsty for the first time.

"I see. I'm thirsty, too." said the mouse.

Waving its tail the scorpion replied,

"Of course! Because everyone is thirsty in the desert!
But not in the forest."

The mouse was curious.

"Then what are you doing here?
If the forest is so nice, why not go there?"

"What? Why not go there?"

After asking the mouse back in a loud voice,
the scorpion slowly lowered its head.

"There is a stream flowing in the forest, but…"

"But?"

The scorpion waved its claws again.

"What if it's scary, terrible, and strange?"

The scorpion covered its face with its claws.

"Being thirsty is better than being scared.
At least I'm used to being thirsty…"

"That's nonsense," said the mouse.

The scorpion shook its body and
splashed the mouse with sand.

The scorpion shouted,

"If you want to go to the forest, go alone!
Don't put me in danger."

"No, that's not what I'm trying to..."

The scorpion raised its tail again and puffed its venom sac.

"You dare try to tempt me? Fat chance!
I am a scorpion, king of the desert!"

Then the scorpion buried and hid itself in the sand.

The mouse was dumbfounded
and stared blankly at the pile of sand
where the scorpion had vanished.

The King of the Desert

However, a second later
the scorpion's tail popped out of the sand
and pointed in the opposite direction.

And then a small voice said,

"Go that way. You'll smell water."

The tail disappeared into the sand and never came back.

The mouse slowly turned around
and started running in the direction the scorpion pointed.
To the forest where a stream flows.

Now he, too, was very thirsty.

IV

 A Fierce Guy

IV

Pant, pant.

After running and running,
the sandscape that the mouse thought
would never end began to change.

He saw large pebbles, stones, and green grass sticking out
from the dirt covering the dark ground.

The grass grew larger and larger into trees.
A narrow, shallow, and clear stream of water
appeared like magic.

"So, this is a stream. That's what it means to flow."

IV

He sat by the clear stream
and drank the cool, refreshing water.
Then he saw his reflection in the water.

Long snout, big ears, and reddish fur.
Thick and long tail.
He was no longer a mouse, but a big fox.

The fox, pleased with its larger body,
walked up the stream.

The trees were now bigger and thicker,
and the sounds of birds and crickets came
from all around.

IV

All the while, with his fox's instinct
he sensed the sound of footsteps creeping up behind him.

"Who is there?"

It was following and matching the fox's steps
to hide the sound of itself stepping on the leaves.

Then suddenly *whoosh!*

"Roar!"

The fox, who had been on alert,
quickly dodged to the side.

"Grrrrr..."

Having failed in its first attack,
it now stood in front of the fox
baring its sharp teeth.

IV

"Fox! You swine! How dare you show up here!"

The roaring coyote's eyes were murderous.

The fox was shaking.
He also felt like this when he saw a shark
at a distance in the sea.
It was an emotion he couldn't identify at that time.
The emotion was fear.

The fox found it hard to control his intimidated body,
but he managed to ask the coyote,

"Isn't this a forest?"

"Yes, it is! And I'm the owner of it!"

The coyote showed its fangs again and growled.

"I'll kill you!"

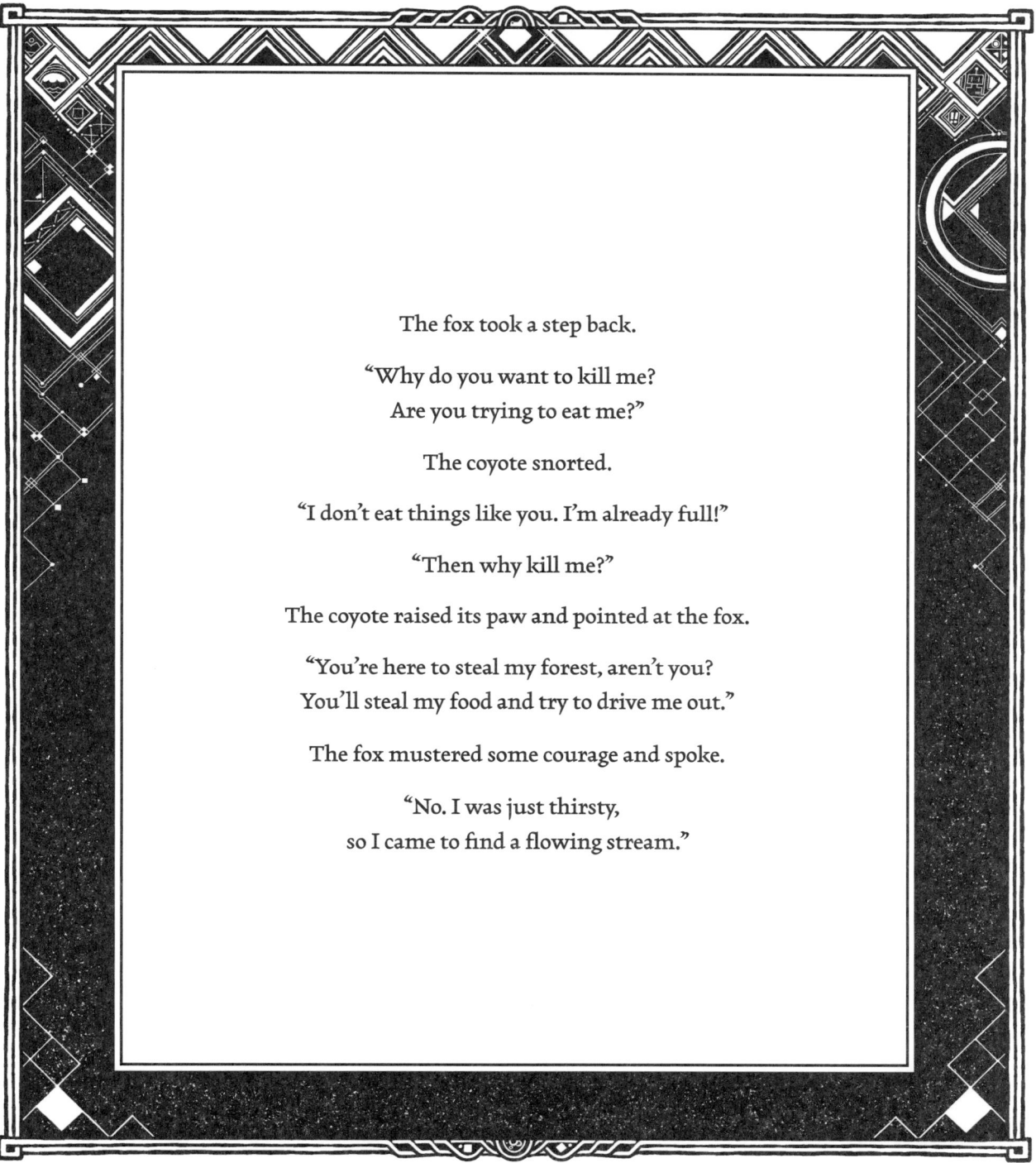

The fox took a step back.

"Why do you want to kill me?
Are you trying to eat me?"

The coyote snorted.

"I don't eat things like you. I'm already full!"

"Then why kill me?"

The coyote raised its paw and pointed at the fox.

"You're here to steal my forest, aren't you?
You'll steal my food and try to drive me out."

The fox mustered some courage and spoke.

"No. I was just thirsty,
so I came to find a flowing stream."

The coyote growled again.

"Don't be ridiculous.
You will go for my neck the moment I fall asleep!"

"I won't do that."

"Everyone does that. First, they pretend to be my friend,
but they hide their evil intentions.
They all just want to take over this forest!"

The coyote fiercely jumped at the fox again.

IV

"Are you really trying to hurt me?"

The fox's blood glistened on the coyote's fangs.

"Of course. Unless you get out of my forest."

And the coyote opened its mouth again,
preparing to attack the fox.

The fox quickly waved his front paw.

"Wait! I'm not going to stay in this forest."

IV

The coyote half closed its mouth.

"You won't stay? Why not?"

"What do you mean by why not?
I didn't intend to stay to begin with."

"But this is a forest with a flowing stream!
You'll never be thirsty.
The trees block the hot sun in the summer.
And in the winter, the spaces between the rocks and caves
block the icy wind."

The fox responded, "So?"

The coyote said in frustration,

"There are lots of prey like squirrels and rabbits,
so you'll never starve. And still, you won't fight me
and try to take over this place?

The coyote kept its fierce eyes on the fox.

The fox answered,

"I have no intention of staying here and
I don't intend to fight you."

The coyote, who had been staring at the fox for a while,
knew that he meant what he said.

IV

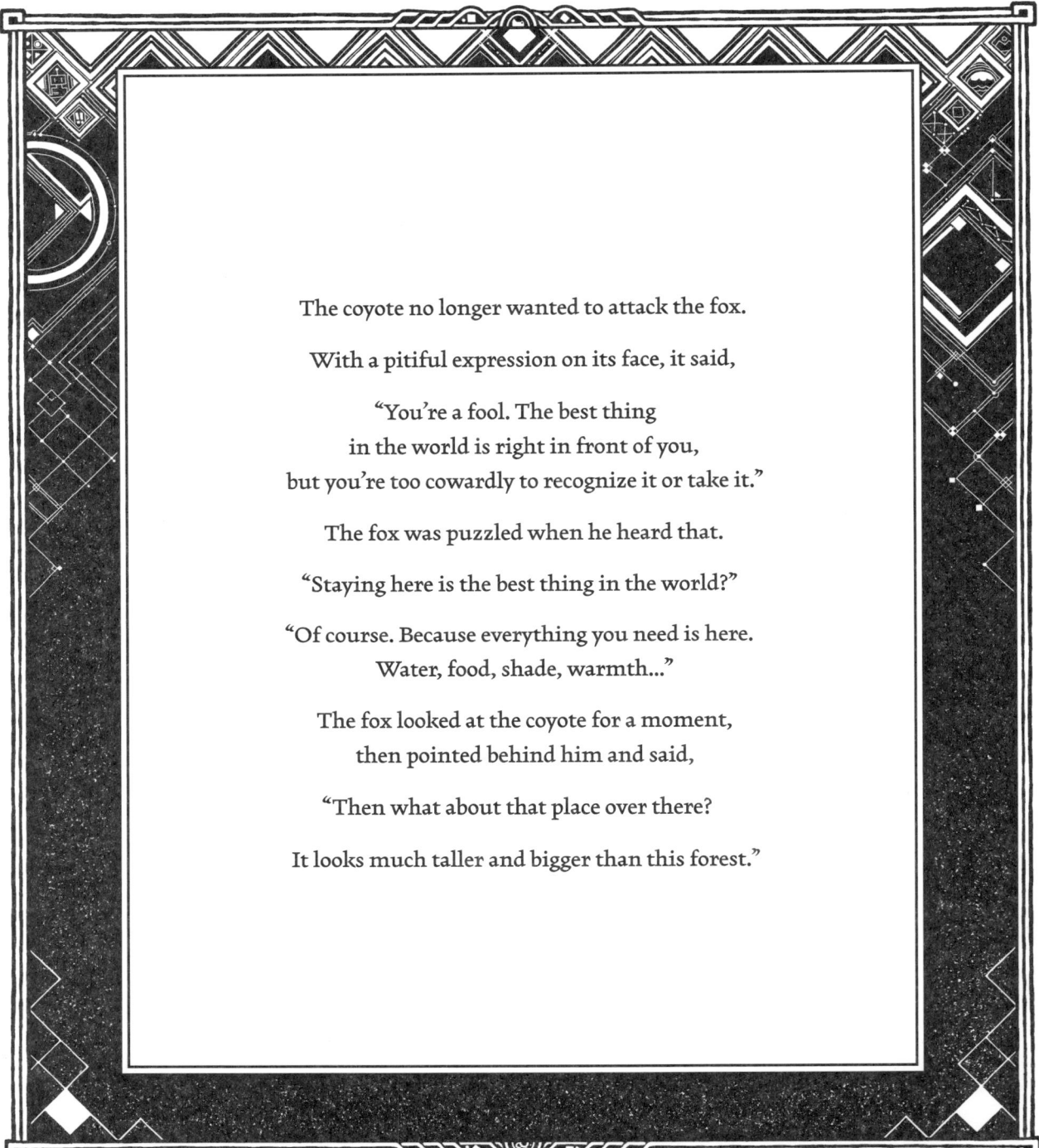

The coyote no longer wanted to attack the fox.

With a pitiful expression on its face, it said,

"You're a fool. The best thing
in the world is right in front of you,
but you're too cowardly to recognize it or take it."

The fox was puzzled when he heard that.

"Staying here is the best thing in the world?"

"Of course. Because everything you need is here.
Water, food, shade, warmth..."

The fox looked at the coyote for a moment,
then pointed behind him and said,

"Then what about that place over there?

It looks much taller and bigger than this forest."

A Fierce Guy

Without even looking at the mountain,
the coyote laughed.

"Haha. You really want to climb that mountain?
Do you think you can go somewhere
I don't even dare to go?"

"Why can't you go?"

The coyote seemed annoyed.

"Why? Because this forest is the best place in the world!
There is water, food, and shade..."

The fox interrupted him.

"I think all those things are over there, plus more."

"Sure. It's full of big animals
that can swallow you whole!"

IV

"You're only a little larger than me,
so they can swallow you whole too, right?"

"I'll never go into the mountains, so it doesn't matter!
You, on the other hand..."

As the fox listened to the Coyote,
he felt something slowly welling up in his chest.

"You said you'd kill me if I stayed here.
I think it'd be better to go
to the mountain rather than die here."

"Why tell me that
the best things in the world are here
when you won't even share them?
And why laugh at me like I am a coward?" said the fox.

"That's..."

"Are you afraid that someone small like me will drink
all the water from that stream?
Are you afraid that I'll eat all the squirrels and rabbits
that are supposed to be your food?"

The feeling of injustice welled up inside the fox.

The fox argued,

"I wasn't planning on staying anyway,
but now I really have to leave.
So you won't get to kill me."

The coyote looked at the fox quietly.

"Do you think I'll pretend to be your friend and then kill you
and take what's yours?
Have you met many animals like that?"

The coyote answered in a weak voice.

"Yes. Many times. And one of them…"

The fox raised its front paw and interrupted the coyote.

"Did they? How are you any different from them?
You tried to kill me as soon as we met."

IV

Now the fox was thirsty,
hungry,
and resentful.

So he became lonely.

"Move, stupid."

The coyote stood blankly as the fox passed.
Then the fox began running toward
the ridge in the distance.

V

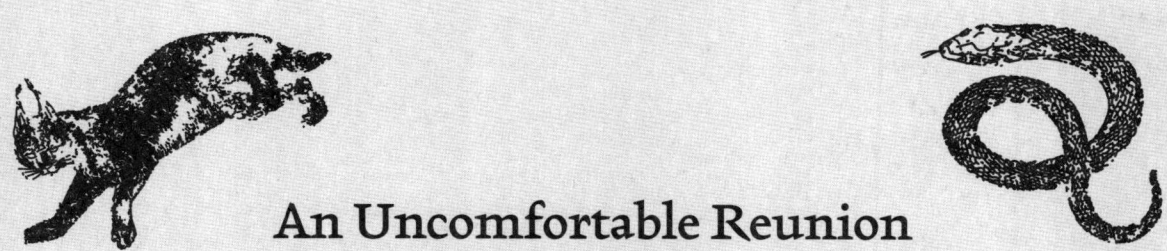

An Uncomfortable Reunion

The mountain was distant
and now, transformed into a wildcat,
it took a long time to arrive at the mountain ridge.

The land was steep, the trees dense and
the roots intertwined with stones
kept getting caught in his small feet.

Even with a light and swift body, it wasn't easy to climb.

But there was a small valley connecting to a brook.

He was able to wet his throat,
so even though he was starving, he could endure.

V

But as the sky darkened to dusk,
his energy gradually waned.

But the top was still far off
and it was getting increasingly harder underfoot.

Other than heading up or down,
he couldn't tell which way was which.

Although he left the forest with a loud boast
when he heard the sad weeping of some beast,
he knew why the coyote didn't go to the mountain.

An Uncomfortable Reunion

V

Even though he spent so much time
as a bubble in the limitless and pitch-black darkness,
even one night on this small mountain
made him afraid of the dark,
so the wildcat slowly silenced the sound of his footsteps.

Crunch-Crunch.

Something alerted him with the sound
of crunching dry leaves and, *GWAK*, breaking branches
but the wildcat continued to climb the mountain.

Then seeing the branches wriggle alive in front of his eyes
surprised, he froze on the spot.

An Uncomfortable Reunion

Sssssssss.

When it ran into the wildcat,
the long snake was slithering along somewhere.

"Oh, shit!"

The snake, annoyed, spat out a curse
as it raised its head and stared at the wildcat.

But the wildcat knew in just one glance
that the moving branches in front of him
was in fact his friend who left the sea in search of land.

It was the eel!

"Wow! You really made it to land!"

The wildcat was so happy to see his friend
that he shouted loudly.

But the snake didn't look happy to see him at all.

The snake stared at the wildcat
with an unpleasant look on its face.

"I'm the fish you met at sea! Remember?"

"You're a fish? We met at sea? Me?"

"Yes! When you were alone and lost your way!"

The snake was confused.

"But I've never been to the ocean."

"But it must've been you!
There's no other animal that looks like you!"

An Uncomfortable Reunion

V

The wildcat came up to the snake and tried to hug him.

But the snake slithered backward and stuck out
its triangle head, exposing its sharp, venomous teeth.

"*Hiss-* Don't get near me!"

The snake's eyes were fierce
and its two fangs were long and sharp.

Because of the snake's force,
the wildcat had no option but to step back.

An Uncomfortable Reunion

V

"You don't remember me?"

The snake responded coldly.

"I know. You're the violent wildcat that tries to eat me."

"That's... But you're the eel!"

The snake sighed.

The wildcat put out his two front paws
he tried to hug the snake with
and looked at the snake for a moment and said,

"You... Changed."

"But considering you followed your destiny,
it'd be strange if you remembered the ocean.
Now you're living out of the water.
And your face has changed a bit."

While the wildcat was talking,
there was a rumbling sound that came from his stomach.

When the snake heard
the sound it slithered a bit back and said,

"How can you say you were a fish with
the way you look now?
Isn't it you who has changed?
Aren't you trying to stick me inside your stomach,
trying to eat me?"

"Yes, it's true. I'm super hungry now.
But I don't eat my friends."

From the snake's point of view,
it was clear that the wildcat had something wrong with his head.

Instead of filling his stomach with something easy to eat
that was right in front of his face,
he kept saying weird things like, "we're friends."

"I have to chase this crazy dude away."

V

The snake played stupid.

He put the tip of his eyes down and said
as pitifully as he could,

"Actually, I lost my memory.
I don't know where I'm from or why I'm here.
I might be from the sea, just like you say."

The wildcat's eyes began to shine.

"That's right. You're my friend, the eel."

"But I lost my memory.
So right now you look like a scary beast.
You can't get rid of that instinctual fear. You understand?"

"Well, yes. But..."

The snake interrupted the wildcat.

"The mountain is a scary place. When it's dusk,
big, ferocious beasts will come out and wander about."

V

An Uncomfortable Reunion

Then, by chance,
scary cries were heard in the distance.

More frightening and loud than anything
the wildcat had ever heard.

"Did you hear that? It's a pack of wolves.
Each one is probably ten times your size.
I can avoid them by hiding inside
the cracks between stones, but you…"

Beside himself, the wildcat began to shake.

The snake looked at him and said,

"By the way, you're just as scary to me
as those wolves are to you!
So please just leave. For the both of us."

"Leave? But where will I go?"

"If you head around the ridge, there's a flat road.
If you cross the road, you'll see a light below."

"A light?"

"Right. A light brighter than all the stars.
Don't fear. Just keep heading down toward the light."

"What do you call it?"

The snake flicked its tongue and said,

"It's called a city. There's a lot to eat and it's a much more abundant place than this mountain."

V

The wildcat's face lit up.

"Really? Okay, then I'll go there.
But, will we ever meet again?"

"Of course. We're old pals."

With a smile on his face,
the wildcat moved toward where the snake directed.

While watching the wildcat, the snake thought,

"I know where you're headed.
Even if you want to come back, you won't be able to."

VI

 Land of Lights

VI

Going down the ridge as the snake instructed,
suddenly a dark black and flat road appeared.

In the sea, desert, forest, mountains,
this was a road unseen before,
wide and somehow strange.

Now transformed into a rust-colored lesser panda,
he followed the road

gently pawing the black surface with his front feet.

Like stone and dirt, not knowing whether
good or bad, it was a strange sensation.

Out of curiosity, while probing the surface of the road a bright light appeared coming from faraway.

Gradually the light became bigger and after a while split into two. What a strange thing to look at. But,

He froze up for a moment and then
in an instant he jumped out of the way and off the road
as the light passed him with a huge *whoosh*.

With his two front feet wrapped around his head,
he lay for a while face down on the ground.

Even the coyote's teeth which wanted to kill him,
the snake's eyes which were cold as ice,
and the cry of the wolf that made his spine shiver,
were not as scary as this.

At least he could talk to each of them
about what they wanted from each other.

VI

But this light
rushed at him with brute force without giving pause.

Whatever you needed,
whatever story you had, it didn't care.

With an unforgiving attitude, it pressed
on whether or not you got in the way.

"But why....?"

He wondered as he lay there
and as his nerves began to settle,
he gradually lifted his body off the ground.

And then, another pair of lights
came from the opposite direction this time.

But he hid from the road before they came.

From a distance it looked like there was a large,
dark body behind the light.

It also appeared as if something was inside it,
but because it moved so fast,
it was impossible to take a closer look.

"Why didn't the eel tell me about this monster?"

The lesser panda was curious,
but didn't want to go back and ask.

Maybe because the lesser panda has a curious instinct
he was ready to get going forward.

VI

"Is this the place where I should cross?"

He guessed at the distance.

As long as he ran when he didn't see light coming
in either direction

it should be possible to cross without difficulty.

"But are those the only kinds of lights?

What if ones that are faster and bigger suddenly appear?"

He worried for a moment, but then
across the road he ran
the soles of his two feet flying as fast as they could go.

Luckily no light was heading toward him at that time and
there were small trees growing across the street.

This was incomparable
to the lights he saw on the road.

There were at least thousands.

The lights were uncountable. Brilliant.

Some were moving on the ground and
some were blinking in the sky.

And the sounds made their way from afar,
like they had order, were well-organized,
and complicated,

and not like crying or laughing or screaming or roaring,
completely different from anything he heard before
all the sounds around him were ringing.

VI

As if he was possessed
he trudged down toward the city.

After the trees vanished
he found himself on a road that was smaller
than the black flat one he had first seen.

Not forgetting what frightened him before,
he avoided the double lights
and entered a street lined with houses.

There were strange tall animals
walking around in groups.

Because he didn't want to face the large animals
he made himself small and walked hidden in the shadows.

VI

While looking for something along the ground,
he ran into a small face.

A chubby bird tottering around on two legs.

While looking at the lesser panda,
the pigeon said despondently,

"Don't even think about eating me.
I'll show you where the food is."

The pigeon motioned with its head
for the lesser panda to follow
and took the lead.

The lesser panda was very hungry.

So even though he thought he should maybe try hunting,
he decided to trust the pigeon instead.

After walking around several alleyways
under a wall in the dark was a telephone pole
and several plates of food.

"Try this. It's healthy. And when you eat it,
there's no blood."

He looked inside the bowl
and saw that it was filled
with many small pebbles that smelled good.

When he took a bite, it was crunchy and super delicious.

"Good, no? It's food for stray cats. But there's a lot of it,
so I eat it, and magpies eat it too."

The lesser panda didn't respond to the pigeon.

He was too busy woofing down the food.

However, while the lesser panda was eating,
he suddenly heard a husky voice coming from behind him.

"What are you?"

He was so distracted while he was eating,
the panda didn't notice that someone had come up to him.

It was a stray cat with a missing eye.

"What? Oh, I...."

The pigeon winked and answered for the lesser panda.

"This guy? He came down from the mountain.
I said he could have some of our food
because we had some left."

"Yes, well."

Seemingly annoyed at the situation,
the stray cat waddled up to another bowl
and slowly started to eat.

Just then, several of the tall animals appeared
in the middle of the road.

Startled, the lesser panda stopped eating
and quickly hid behind the telephone pole.

The lesser panda asked, "What are they? They're so big...."

The pigeon's eyes opened wide.

"What? You don't know humans?
You must've been really deep in the mountains."

"Humans?"

The stray cat finished eating his food
and looked at the lesser panda.

"It's humans that put this food out for us everyday."

"That's right! Even though I usually eat here,
over there at the public square
people give us pigeons food too."

VI

The lesser panda was truly in awe.

"That's wild. Up until now all the animals
I've met were only worried about losing their food,
but these animals they hand out food willingly."

"That's right. That's humans for you."

Then turning back from the darkness it vanished into,
in a low voice the cat said,

"And it's also humans who made my eye like this."

VII

 Happy Sleep

VII

"Why...?"

As soon as the stray cat vanished, everyone slowly left
and now he transformed into a small dog,
alone, in the dark alleyway.

The story about humans was strange.

Why if they were feeding animals
were they also hurting them?

Every animal he ever met,
even the ones that tried to eat him
were not like that.

But for some reason the dog didn't hate humans.

The dog wanted to meet humans,
wanted to know them.

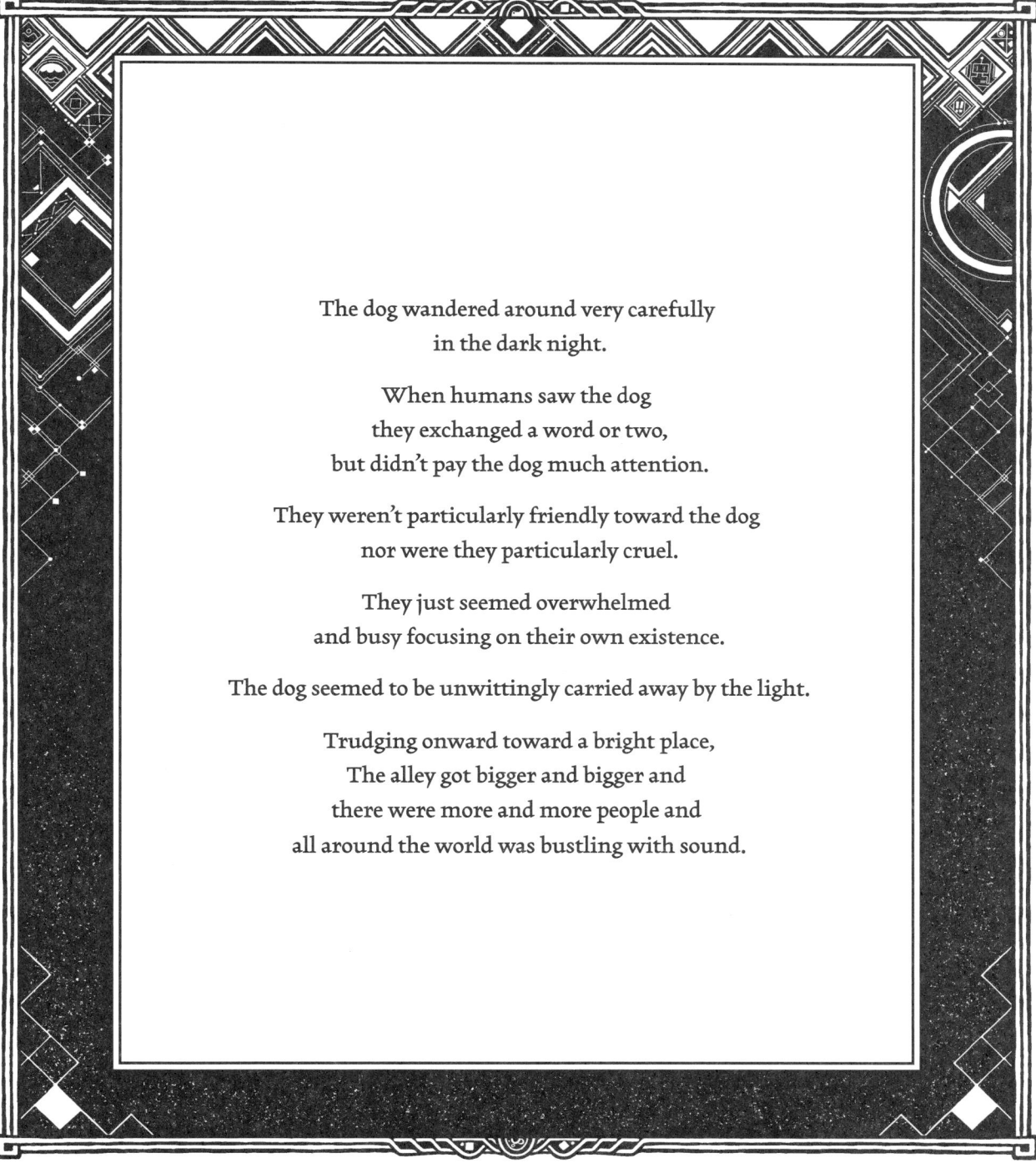

The dog wandered around very carefully
in the dark night.

When humans saw the dog
they exchanged a word or two,
but didn't pay the dog much attention.

They weren't particularly friendly toward the dog
nor were they particularly cruel.

They just seemed overwhelmed
and busy focusing on their own existence.

The dog seemed to be unwittingly carried away by the light.

Trudging onward toward a bright place,
The alley got bigger and bigger and
there were more and more people and
all around the world was bustling with sound.

VII

But coming from some corner
the dog heard a different sound pierce through the noise.

Chiming, winding, silky sounds.
And between them, a human's voice.

It was as high as the sound of a crying wolf,
but not scary at all, so the dog trundled along
toward the place where the sound came from.

And in front of the person making the sound
the dog sat, wagging his tale.

Happy Sleep

VII

When the human saw
the wide-eyed dog sitting in front of him
she stopped singing and
sat down in front of the dog and asked,

"And who are you?"

The dog wanted to respond.

"Woof, woof!"

But the dog was not able to make
the sounds of a human voice,
so only barks came out.

Up until now he could talk to all different kinds of animals
and he could understand what humans said, so it was weird.

"Are you hungry?"

"(No!) Woof! Woof!"

Looking at the dog for a moment
the person carefully stuck out her hand
and petted the dog's head.

The dog appreciated the person's touch
and feeling toward him.

He wagged his tail without realizing he was doing it.
The human laughed at the dog.

People passing by on the street saw the dog and the human
and smiled and started to stop.

"Because of you people are coming.
Now I feel like I've got some mojo.
I'll start singing again."

The winding, silky sounds began again
as the human started to pluck the strings.

And a clear song could be heard again.

The dog sat quietly in front of the human
and listened to the song.

A story about love,
a story about dreams,
a story about forgotten things,
the human looked at the dog
once in a while as she sang the songs.

More spectators came
and several of the audience members pet the dog
and placed variously colored paper
in the guitar case in front of the human playing the guitar.

VII

After listening to the songs for a while,
the night grew long and cold.

"I can't play anymore, my hands are cold stiff."

As if talking to herself, the human talked to the dog,
finished the song, and began packing up the guitar.

"Where did you come from?"

"Woof! Woof!"

"Do you want to come with me?
Tomorrow we can try to find your owner."

"Woof! Woof!"

The human slung the guitar case,
which was as big as she was,
over her back and started to walk away.
The dog followed.

The two of them went down the dark alley.
There were fewer and fewer people there.
It grew so quiet it was completely silent.

VII

The human went into a basement.

The door creaked
and the room was cold and small even for the two of them.

But the dog liked it anyway.

"We'll stay here just for tonight, okay?"

"Woof! Woof!"

The human put her bag down
and sat back in a corner of the room.

The bright light that filled the human's face
when she sang began to disappear
and fatigue started to take its place.

Happy Sleep

VII

"I should wash up and go to sleep…"

The human mumbled and lay down
in the corner of the room.
Then suddenly the dog heard a heavy sigh and quiet breathing.

The dog inspected the human quietly.

What kind of love and longing were contained in those songs?

He had been alone all this time
wondering here and there, finally ending up in this world.
Were the feelings in the song like this feeling?

And being right here, living it all again
from the sea to the desert
to the forest to the mountain to the city,
and finally being here in this room,
perhaps it was like this feeling?

But why is this human's heart
not filled with love?

Why does she fall asleep alone like that?

The dog approached the human and smelled her.
Soft skin, lotion, and a bit of sweat.
Without realizing it,
the dog found himself licking the human's face.

Even though the human wasn't as complete
as some of the other animals,
the dog found this human to be absolutely loveable.

The dog entered the human's arms
and rolled up his body.

Just like that, he was warm
even though the room was cold.

VIII

 Awakening

He had a dream.

He was a bubble again in his dream.
But this time he wasn't small.

He became a huge bubble
with a luminous bright light
coming down to envelop the whole blue world.

He saw himself inside of it.

An unknowing fish swimming.

A mouse who did nothing but run.

A fox that bled.

A wildcat who endured hunger and met a friend.

A lesser panda rolling around on a jet-black road.

And a good dog that just fell asleep.

VIII

All the animals that he met,
he met again in the dream.

The eel who knew nothing,
who suffered from losing its way.

The scorpion that became violent because it was scared.

The coyote who killed friends
because it was afraid of being betrayed.

A snake who was manipulative
and poisonous because it was weak.

"Yes, actually he wasn't an eel.
That's just the way I wanted to see him."

A pigeon that gave up flying and
a stray cat who gave up hope and
living in pain day by day.

Awakening

Then he finally met humans.

At first he was scared of them,
but it turns out they're just tall,
and the truth is that they aren't really that big.

In that great height is a small heart curled up
just like a fish, like a scorpion, like a mouse, like a fox,
like a wildcat, like a lesser panda, just like a dog.

All got thirsty, got hungry,
and wanted to feel warmth.

Everyone is not that different.
Just as a bubble follows light in the infinite darkness,
they all want to search for their own light.

Now it's time to wake up.

The white rhino slowly lifted his body up.

Why did he have to be in such a long silence and why did he come here?

Why did he fall asleep and wake up again?

After experiencing a world where everything exists, now he understood.

Those bubbles gradually bunched
and became one giant bubble. Then the white rhino
started walking again with the bubble on his back.

Even though nothing that exists, not even the rhino
is perfect or eternal,
just to find one's place and walk forward with all your strength,
is the truth he knows now, a light he can share.

Those who walk like that can create new worlds, and
in those worlds
they can wash everyone's fear, wounds, worries, and pain away.

Some things can't be erased, some can't be forgotten,
but if they can be washed away, then we can start over.

The light isn't out there somewhere, in some faraway place.
It's inside everyone.

The white rhino
that has experienced the infinite and the finite,
is now ready to take the lead and step
into that light.

The Dream of the White Rhino: For Freedom in the Meta Universe

Publication date	January 1, 2024
Text	Won Jongwoo
Illustrations	Kim Kibeom
Art Direction	Seo Junsu
Design	Ok Yirang
English Translation	Jake Levine, Soohyun Yang
Planning and Production	Galaxy Corporation Co., Ltd.
Address	10, Gukjegeumyung-ro, Yeongdeungpo-gu, Seoul, Republic of Korea Three IFC 53F
Web	www.galaxyuniverse.ai
For inquiries	elin@galaxyuniverse.ai

© 2024 Galaxy Corporation Co., Ltd. All rights reserved.

The rights of this book are held by Galaxy Corporation. This publication may only be reproduced, stored, or transmitted in any form, or by any means, with written consent of the copyright holder.